Barn Style Homes

Design Ideas for Timber Frame Houses

Tina Skinner & Tony Hanslin

Schiffer ®
Publishing Ltd

4880 Lower Valley Road, Atglen, PA 19310 USA

Library of Congress Cataloging-in-Publication Data

Skinner, Tina.
Barn style homes : design ideas for timber frame
houses / Tina Skinner & Tony Hanslin.
p. cm.
ISBN 0-7643-1319-3
1. wooden-frame houses--Design. I. Hanslin, Tony. II.
Title.
NA7173 .S58 2001
728'.37--dc21
00-012434

Designed by Bonnie M. Hensley
Cover design by Bruce M. Waters
Type set in Zurich LtCn BT/Zurich BT

ISBN: 0-7643-1319-3
Printed in China

Cover and title page photos © 2000 Suki Coughlin/Paula
McFarland stylist

Copyright and page 3 photos © 2000 Suki Coughlin/Paula
McFarland stylist

Published by Schiffer Publishing Ltd.
4880 Lower Valley Road
Atglen, PA 19310
Phone: (610) 593-1777; Fax: (610) 593-2002
E-mail: Schifferbk@aol.com
Please visit our web site catalog at **www.schifferbooks.com**

In Europe, Schiffer books are distributed by Bushwood Books
6 Marksbury Avenue Kew Gardens
Surrey TW9 4JF England
Phone: 44 (0) 20-8392-8585; Fax: 44 (0) 20-8392-9876
E-mail: Bushwd@aol.com
Free postage in the UK. Europe: air mail at cost.

This book may be purchased from the publisher.
Include $3.95 for shipping. Please try your bookstore first.
We are always looking for people to write books on new and related subjects.
If you have an idea for a book please contact us at the Atglen, PA address.
You may write for a free catalog.

Contents

Acknowledgements

Like so many of the homeowners who built these houses, I have seen Yankee Barn Homes advertised in countless magazines, and lingered over the images. Immersed in other projects, I took a moment to visit the company's website one day, and impulsively purchased their design guide, thinking it might contribute to a book project one day down the line.

Well, once contacted, the friendly folks at Yankee Barn Homes will do all they can to be helpful. In my case, I told them I was only a book writer at this time, not a homebuilder. And before a month had passed, the company's Chief Executive Tony Hanslin was on my doorstep (a very out of the way place) ready to discuss how he could help me with a book on post and beam construction.

Not only could he help, it turns out that Yankee Barn Homes has been amassing a wonderful collection of images from the customized homes they've helped people design and build. More than I could squeeze between two covers. I think the best of the images are here, as well as helpful floor plans, most of which the home designers had to recreate for this publication. To them, to Inge Smith who coordinated the whole effort, and to Tony, many thanks.

Finally, it wouldn't be fair to send this book off to press without acknowledging the work of Tammy Ward, who scanned all the floor plans and typed in the room names and dimensions. Her careful work made this book more complete.

Introduction

In this modern day and age, the highest technology has created housing materials that allow an air-tight exterior so light you can punch your way into the house. In fact, many stick-built homes are constructed this way today, with foam board forming the outside wall, air space between beams, and plasterboard on the inside.

So it's no wonder that we dream of old-fashioned houses, built of solid timbers. Real wood is a warm and comforting presence in our lives, a connection to nature, and beautiful in its own right. Post and beam construction will last for untold years to come. In fact, Yankee Barn Homes, the company that provided the images for this book, uses reclaimed beams that have already spent over 100 years holding up sturdy mills. Long since past their infancy as structural materials, well beyond the long drying and shrinking process, these strong timbers give new housing a sense of timelessness and inherent antiquity. And they stand as their own form of art, whether framing picture windows or original artworks, serving as hangers for copper pots and pans in the kitchen, or punctuating the transition from one great open room to another.

A post and beam frame provides tremendous design flexibility when planning a new house. It is unlike traditional "stick-built" construction, where the walls support the house. With post and beam construction the timber frame carries most of the weight. Interior walls can be non-structural and moved around within the house.

These homes draw their inspiration from an architectural tradition that pre-dates the United States; from church and barn structures that still stand in Europe today. As you look at these homes, you may be reminded of classic countryside structures such as bank barns, English barns, Yankee barns, and round barns. In fact, the owners of these homes take pride in the fact that their houses seem part of the landscape rather than garish new additions.

This book showcases beautiful homes, designed by the owners in cooperation with Yankee Barn Homes. Each has its unique personality, though most share a common goal: a warm and inviting home that serves both as a quiet retreat for the owners, and an elegant place to entertain family and friends.

The images in this book are packed with design ideas both for house structure and for decorating ideas for the timber-frame or refurbished barn owner. It will prove invaluable for people looking for ideas for furnishing their great room, decorating a fireplace, and situating furniture to encompass great views while creating nooks for conversation and relaxation.

Feeling of Home

When planning a new retirement home, this couple wasn't quite ready to give up their historic home's ambience. That's why they opted for a home style rich with wooden beams. In designing the home, they kept their living areas similar to what they were leaving in order to accommodate their furniture, and ease the transition. The result is an elegant new home rich with memories and family treasures.

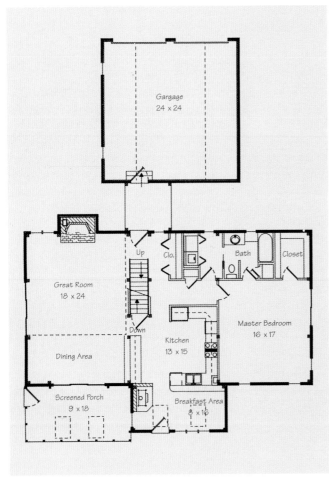

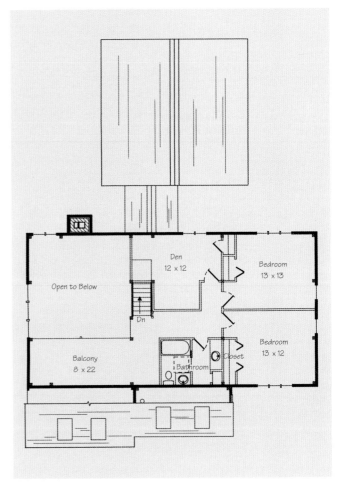

The homeowners wanted a large kitchen to accommodate family and friends. Just off the kitchen, a warm, cozy area was furnished with a woodstove.

Because their son and daughter-in-law are artists, the owners wanted wall space to hang large pieces of art. The balcony overlooking the great room was also furnished to allow for the pursuit of another art, this one musical.

"We wanted a light, open, airy home with lots of glass. We didn't want rooms. We wanted different living areas open to each other," the owner said.

Guest bedrooms were situated upstairs while the master bedroom is conveniently located on the first floor.

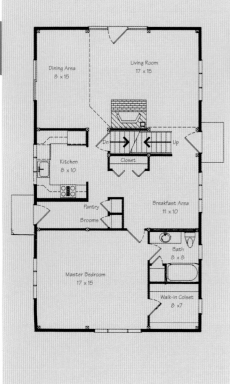

Dining Area
8 x 15

Living Room
17 x 15

Dn   Up

Closet

Kitchen
8 x 10

Breakfast Area
11 x 10

Pantry

Brooms

Bath
8 x 8

Master Bedroom
17 x 15

Walk-in Colset
8 x7

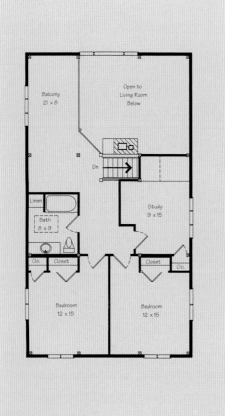

Balcony
21 x 8

Open to
Living Room
Below

Dn

Linen

Bath
8 x 9

Study
9 x 15

Clo.   Closet

Closet   Clo.

Bedroom
12 x 15

Bedroom
12 x 15

A Contemporary Barn

After living in many old houses, these homebuilders had their hearts set on something with a contemporary flair. The home had to take advantage of a lot with a sweeping view over a lake in upstate New York, uncomplicated and with clean lines. They chose a simple barn-like structure to blend into the surrounding countryside, and designed the interior so that every room has a sight-line to the lake nearby.

Photo credit: © Suki Coughlin

A light staining on antique beams and a smooth white plaster coating on the chimney helps create a contemporary look. The homeowners wanted walls that would showcase their collection of original art, and allow for rooms filled with natural light. A cathedral ceiling in the great room has a dramatic effect.

A master bedroom with master bath and walk-in closet were created on the first floor, secluded by the woodlands behind the home.

Cutout areas were incorporated throughout the house to allow light to shine from skylights — here into a hallway — giving the illusion of more open space.

White and wood were married for a completely contemporary kitchen.

Creating Permanent Niches

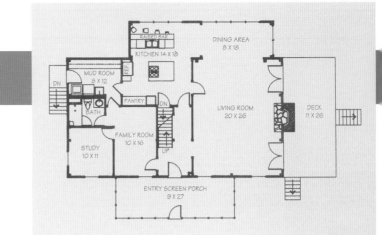

An interior designer and world-traveling Marine wanted to settle down on their lakeside lot in Virginia with a feeling of permanence. Envisioning a place where the family would both mingle and escape to relax, they designed a home with interconnecting rooms with niches for reading, watching sunsets, sharing stories, or catching up with office work.

Photo credit: © 2000 F & E Schmidt

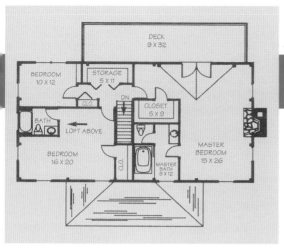

The owners didn't want to lose space upstairs, so they raised the ceiling to 10 feet on the first floor. This kept the living room open and airy while allowing for a master bedroom above.

A fieldstone fireplace helps the home blend into its surroundings, and hides the deck supports. French doors on either side create a bright view of the fireplace inside, and lead the family outdoors to enjoy the deck.

Double-hung windows in the kitchen and dining area take in the lake view and create a feeling that fits into the southern, lakeside setting. The dark timber frame is reminiscent of an English Tudor manor.

The focal point in the master bedroom is a green marble fireplace. The room has a private deck with stunning lake views.

Two guest bedrooms were furnished upstairs to accommodate frequent visitors to this wooded retreat.

These homeowners were looking to capture the quaint look of a summer cottage on the Maine coast, yet enjoy a soaring two-story design. "We wanted to build a traditional summer cottage to fit into the environment, one owner said. She recalled summer vacations on the coast, and the cottages "with their shingles, angles, and great big porches."

The rustic style was accomplished using dormers and a wrap-around porch. Inside, an open floor plan and walls of windows were installed to take advantage of a mountain view to east and south. The unusual design helped win the house the 1996 grand prize in *Country Home Magazine's* annual design contest.

Photo credit: © 2000 F & E Schmidt

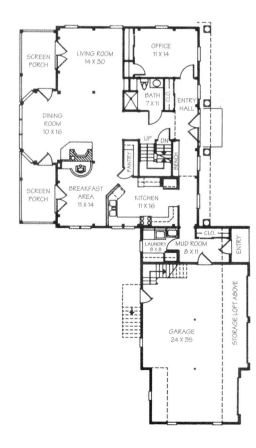

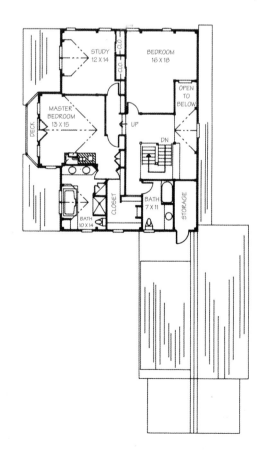

Top left: Being a retirement home, master bedroom suites were planned for both the up- and downstairs. The downstairs room, however, was originally furnished as an office.

Top right: A spare bedroom treats guests to lots of light and air. Spare window treatments add to the effect, while shades can be drawn for privacy.

Inside the entry soars to a cathedral ceiling and visitors have a dramatic view south through the house.

A place to curl up and relax was created off the upstairs master bedroom, with views from the balcony.

The homeowners wanted their kitchen to work as a separate room from the rest of the house, yet to keep the cook in on any conversations transpiring beyond.

The homeowners wanted a high ceiling in the great room to accommodate their grandfather clock and to allow for a master bedroom with a view above.

The dining area commands a bank of
windows, which also filter light to the living
room and the entryway area.

Beams and angles allow for interesting decor
in this small bathroom.

Casual Entertaining

These homeowners rejected the Georgian Colonial home style that dominated the Maryland area where they'd bought a riverfront lot. They wanted something big and open for entertaining, and reflective of their casual lifestyle. The informality of a barn-style home with an open floor plan pleased them.

Photo credit: © Suki Coughlin

A large great room and a big kitchen were top priorities for this home design. The owners enjoy casual entertaining, and they have created a comfortable environment here with rich wood and brick tones reflected in oriental carpeting and velvet furniture.

Photo credit: © Suki Coughlin

Generous-size tubs fit neatly under roof overhangs where headroom is not a priority.

The TV loft provides an airy retreat at the top of the house.

A low, beamed ceiling creates a cozy feel in this guest bedroom.

A loft seating area overlooks the great room.

The furniture is formal, but the space allotted in this dining room allows satiated guests to push back their chairs and enjoy each other and the view beyond.

Roots in the States

After years living abroad, these homebuilders wanted a place they could truly call their own back home. A place where their daughters could finish high school, and where they would return with their own families. Every detail was poured over. Everyone in the family threw in their own two cents. The consensus was that the house must be "awesome."

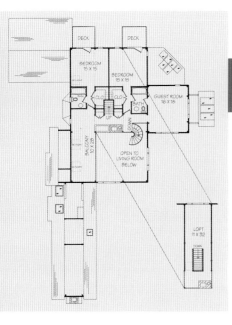

A fieldstone chimney dominates the great room, which is flooded by light from an arched bank of windows.

The kitchen has a his side and a her side. His is complete with a granite surface with utensils and spices since he wears the chef's hat. Her side is more suitable to her baker's cap with a cutting board surface, bins, and a breadbox. They aren't the only two allowed, however. The cooks can visit with guests milling around in the adjacent breakfast area.

Photo credit: © 1993 Suki Coughlin

A separate master bedroom suite includes a sitting area, a private retreat away from guests.

Photo credit: © Suki Coughlin

The homeowners used magazines and books to find ideas, like this window over the Jacuzzi, and then worked them into their plans.

360° Island Views

Besides views of Block Island, the homeowners wanted their windows to provide additional functions. Creative placement of windows adds height to the views and gives his home the look he wanted. "I was inspired by shingle architecture," the owner and designer said. "I wanted a Victorian look for my beach house — French doors, stacked windows, a round-top window, and a notched-in balcony."

For the exterior, a dormer over the balcony opens up the master bedroom beyond and breaks up the exterior line of the house.

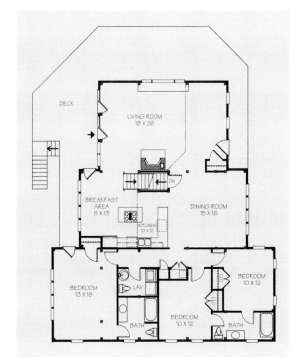

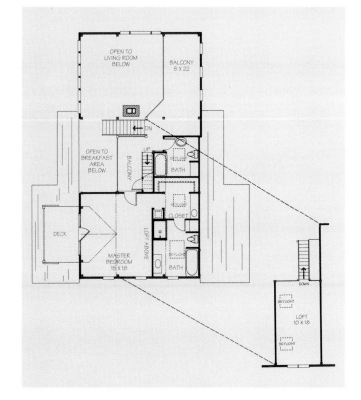

Photo credit: © Suki Coughlin

The master bedroom
commands a view of
the sunrise, as well as
a private elevated
deck for the best
views.

The kitchen is open on both sides. In this image, the breakfast area can be seen framed by stacked windows. Behind the photographer, an equal wall of windows overlooks a larger, more formal dining area.

The living room is open two stories high, with an arched bank of windows soaring above for incredible views of the ocean. A balcony takes advantage of the elevation, placing the viewer above the sand dunes.

The master bath enjoys natural light from a small window and a skylight. Wooden vanity and mirror add rustic charm to the room.

Being at the beach means being outside whenever the weather is clement. A deck wraps around the living areas of the home.

Now That's Living

In planning their dream home overlooking one of the Finger Lakes in upstate New York, these homeowners knew just what they wanted. First of all, they started with the indoor pool, an amenity they'd enjoyed in their previous house. They angled two ells off the main structure in order to make a windbreak for their deck overlooking the lake. For the front approach, they created a more formal look using traditional double-hung windows with oversized glass. This helped break up the long straight line of the front side of the house. To complement this, they used clapboard siding, with vertical siding along the wings.

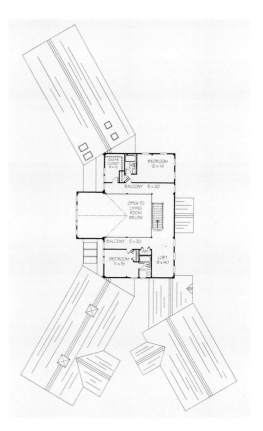

For the pool house, overhead trusses were used rather than posts and beams for support. Glass was included floor-to-ceiling to maximize lake views.

The new homeowner finds it frustrating when people join her in the kitchen while she's preparing a meal, so she designed a large central island to separate the kitchen from the dining room.

Photo credit: © Suki Coughlin

The master bedroom was secluded at the end of a wing. After passing down a hallway, one arrives in an open, light retreat, complete with private deck.

A luxurious soak, this Jacuzzi in the master bath also commands a lake view.

The great room is dominated by a round-top window. Expansive Oriental carpets add warmth to the room, but the furnishings were left spare to accentuate the space and grandeur of the setting.

Photo credit: © Suki Coughlin

A Work of Art

esigned by and for a writer/illustrator, this home is a center for creativity. Though he does his work in a converted barn nearby, the home was also designed to fulfill his creative urges in the cooking, home decorating, and gardening arenas. Weathered barn siding creates a warm grey tone outside, which the owner complemented with splashes of color.

Photo credit: © 1990 Suki Coughlin

Photo credit: © Suki Coughlin

The living room or great hall was given a southwestern flair with terra-cotta tile and Mexican decorations. The walls, beams, and brick fireplace surround were painted white to enhance the collection.

Photo credit: © Suki Coughlin

Photo credit: © Suki Coughlin

The owner loves to cook, and wanted two separate areas to practice his art. He does most of his cooking on a restaurant quality gas stove-top in the kitchen, but he has a whole other area for grilling. Adjacent to the dining area is a small room with a huge grill set in a red brick enclosure. Next to the structure is a double wall oven where he bakes bread.

Photo credit: © 1994 Suki Coughlin

Atlantic Advantage

This family vacation home is poised on a bluff with an incredible view of the Atlantic Ocean. So the back of the home is where the windows are. Besides the expansive living room, which enjoys the two-story round-top window, the owners needed space for family and guests, that sometimes number up to 60 for dinner. Adding a family room in one ell expanded the entertaining space. Another ell was added to create a private master bedroom that still capitalizes on the ocean view.

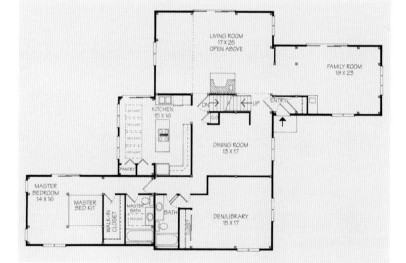

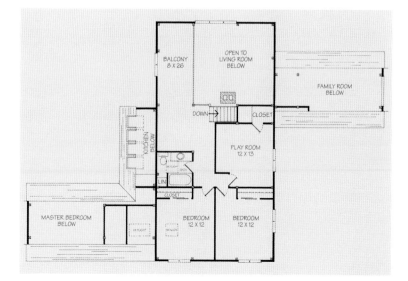

Guests can walk out onto the wrap-around deck from any room in the house.

The owner loves to cook, and wanted walls between her and the guests while she prepares the meals. To satisfy their thirst, a small wet bar and fridge were placed adjacent to the family room for easy access.

Photo credit: © 1994 Suki Coughlin

Photo credit: © 1994 Suki Coughlin

Photo credit: © Suki Coughlin

Photo credit: © 1993 Suki Coughlin

A dark stain on the beams and white wall panels create striking contrasts for the living room.

A master bedroom was tucked into an ell off the main house for privacy.

A formal dining room is used for smaller gatherings; the homeowners often entertain for dinner, sometimes with as many as 60 guests.

Country Comfort

or their vacation retreat, these second home owners wanted cozy coupled with charm. Scale wasn't important, since the space was designated as a place for family get-togethers, not "aparts," though they left room for a soaring ceiling over the living room to make the home feel much bigger than its 2,100 square feet.

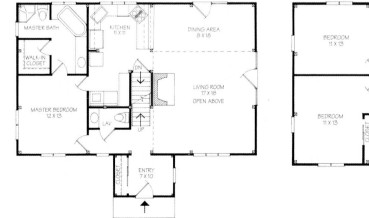

Sunny yellow cabinets and drapes, and a bright, checkerboard tile on floor and walls, create a happy kitchen atmosphere.

The living room was built large, with an overhanging balcony. To keep the scale comfortable, though, the wood walls were stained a rich honey color, and drapes were used to soften the tall round-top window.

Photo by Keith Scott Morton

Photo by Keith Scott Morton

A dining room sits just beyond the kitchen, where a pass-through window also works as buffet counter.

Half of the upstairs overlooks the living quarters, the other half accommodates a guest room and a comfy TV/sitting room.

The master bedroom and bath were, like the rest of the home, richly draped in textiles, wallpaper, and window treatments to create a feeling of comfort and warmth.

A Family Retreat

Designed for a couple of empty nesters planning on frequent visits from children and grandchildren, this house had to be all things to many people. The kitchen was placed as the hub of the weekend retreat, with open living areas branching away from the food. Nooks were created for privacy, including a television/media room, and a master bedroom secluded far from the living areas. Upstairs are enchanting guest rooms, and an upper balcony is a magnet for the grandchildren who want to play amongst themselves.

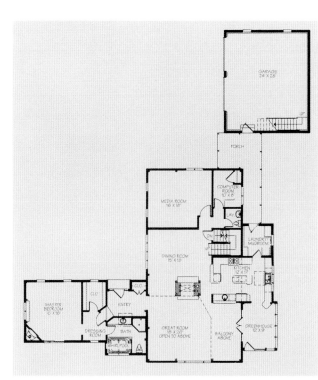

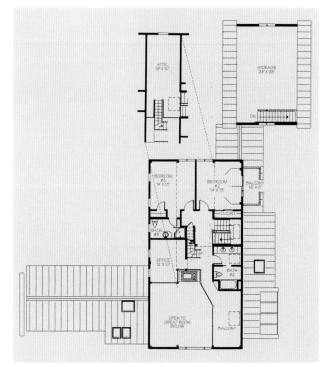

Photo credit: © 1996 Suki Coughlin

The kitchen was designed to be the hub of household activity. It's where people enter the house via a mudroom after romps in the nearby woods. It also opens to a formal dining room, the great room, and a greenhouse/breakfast nook.

Photo credit: © 1996 Suki Coughlin,

Photo credit: © 1996 Suki Coughlin

Photo credit: © 1996 Suki Coughlin

A secluded master's bedroom has a gas fireplace and opens to a patio in the back.

An enormous fieldstone fireplace dominates the great room, which links to the rest of the house.

Rustic Weekends

Low maintenance, high comfort were priorities for this vacation home in the woods. The owners wanted casual rustic charm combined with contemporary living. The wide-open spaces they craved were accomplished by using timber frame trusses to support the roof over the great room, where kitchen, dining areas, and a huge living room were located, uninter-rupted by posts. Built into a hillside, the home design borrows from the classic bank barn concept with a walkout basement, where two extra bedrooms, a family room, and a hot-tub room exist. The exterior is characterized by the vertical shiplap siding set off by the field stone chimney and walls of glass.

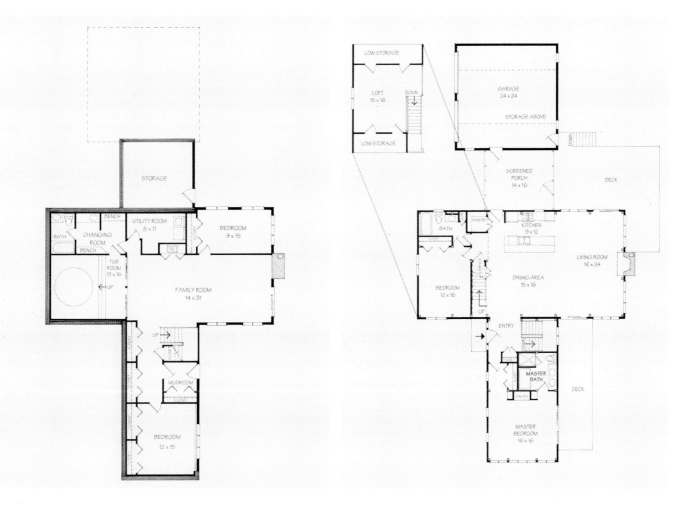

A fieldstone fireplace framed by floor-to-ceiling windows dominates the great room — kitchen, dining area, and living room. To achieve the rustic charm they craved, the owners incorporated planed Douglas Fir beams, wood paneling on the ceilings, and random-width plank floorboards. Area rugs help create zones within the living space.

A first priority upon arrival at the vacation house is heating up the hot tub — the ideal way to unwind from the work-a-day world.

Opposite page
Bottom right: Curtains pull closed at night for privacy in the master bedroom. In the morning, they open to reveal views on three sides of the home.

Feeling Meadow

These homeowners wanted their structure to blend into its surroundings — a beautiful hillside meadow overlooking a pond. They chose a barn-style home because of the history of such designs in the region. In fact, the view from their home includes an old barn and silo in the distance. They wanted lots of glass and light, and something unique that reflected the way they liked to live.

Photo credit: © 2000 Brad Simmons

Floor plan labels (first floor):
Walk-in Closet 10 x 9 · Master Bedroom 13 x 24 · Master Bath 10 x 14 · Bath 8 x 6 · Den 8 x 11 · Great Room 18 x 23 · Foyer 10 x 8 · Dining Room 16 x 17 · Kitchen 16 x 16 · Laundry Room 12 x 8 · Screened Porch 14 x 14 · Garage 23 x 27

Floor plan labels (second floor):
Balcony 8 x 24 · Den Below · Open to Great Room Below · Open to Foyer Below · Balcony · Clo. · Bedroom 10 x 14 · Bath 5 x 10 · Bedroom 10 x 13 · Kitchen Below · Loft 10 x 14

A collection of folk art was snuggled in around a massive fieldstone chimney and antique timbers used in the post and beam construction. Passive solar warmth pours in the through banks of windows, making the home bright and cost efficient to heat during the blustery wintry months on this hillside.

A low ceiling with wood paneling lends an air of intimacy and formality to this dining room which, like much of the home, was furnished with antiques.

A blue wash on the cabinetry creates a feeling of age and informality for the kitchen. A central table with colorful chairs stands as invitation for family and friends to gather here for food and conversation.

A quiet corner, this den opens only to the sky, creating a concentrated area for getting work or, in this case, flytying, done.

The master bedroom and bath stand alone in an ell of the house. A two-tone stain wash on the cabinetry creates an interesting effect in the master bath. A mirror is positioned to take advantage of the view through a window on the opposite wall.

Religious Retreat

A retired clergyman, this home owner had to watch his budget. To do this, he used smaller, standard windows, and sacrificing some of the post and beam frame. Still, his home has the rustic wood, and the soaring feeling, that make him marvel that his home "feels like a cathedral."

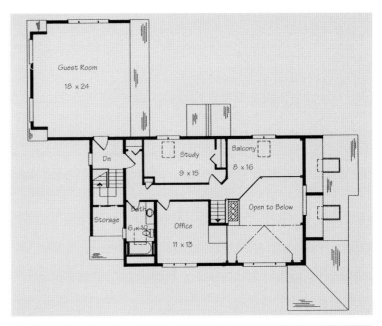

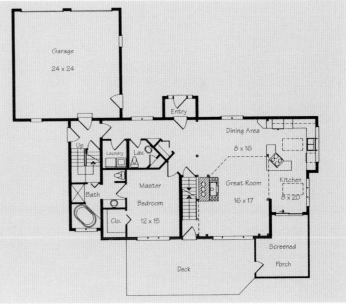

Photo credit: © Suki Coughlin

Photo credit: © Suki Coughlin

Opposite page
A woodstove and reasonable proportions make this "great room" a personal, family gathering center.

His and hers work areas were set up on the second floor (see floor plan), with easy access to a balcony overlooking the whole spread.

Here's the true hangout in any home, the kitchen. In this case it was kept cozy, with a breakfast nook overlooking the woods.

Photo credit: © Suki Coughlin

Photo credit: © Suki Coughlin

A Nice Addition

These homeowners bought an old cape knowing that they'd need to expand it. They liked the idea of a barn-style frame and timber home. The kitchen of the old cape was converted to a hallway leading into the new section of the home. The addition houses the new kitchen, a big family room, and the master bedroom on one level, additional bedrooms upstairs.

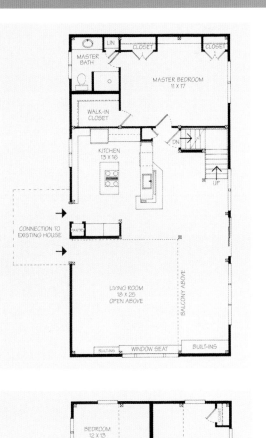

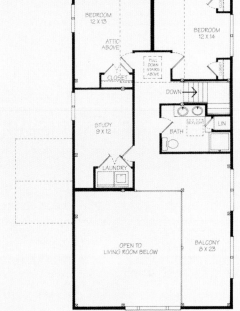

A balcony area overlooking the living room
offers a private place to curl up and read.

A guest bedroom was furnished with a grand-daughter in mind.

The owners are in love with all the light streaming into their main living area. A window seat serves as altar for these sun worshippers.

Lakeside Footprint

When they retired, these homeowners wanted to live in the same place where they'd vacationed for years. They loved the lot, the problem was with the cottage; it was much too small. When they rebuilt, they needed to work on the exact footprint of the cottage. While they were at it, they needed to create enough space for children and grandchildren, and they wanted to create a place that would be used for generations to come. Post and beam architecture allowed them to have an open downstairs and have the accommodations they needed above.

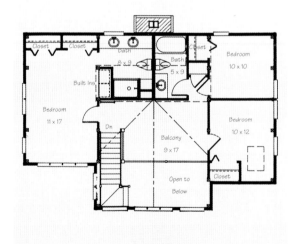

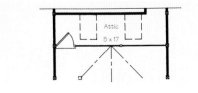

Photo credit: © 1998 Suki Coughlin

A fireplace dominates a living room at the back of the house. Attractive plaids and overstuffed furniture make the large area comfortable and inviting for family gatherings.

A small sitting room faces the lake and opens onto a deck that takes full advantage of the view.

The master bedroom is spacious enough for a king-size bed and a small seating area next to the picture windows.

It may be small, but this little loft is a child magnet and was furnished appropriately for play.

The kitchen cabinetry and floor were stained to match antique timbers.

All About Antiques

Family treasures and auction finds were at the heart of every design decision these homeowners made. They were fully committed to incorporate as much of the past as possible in their new home. They even went out and reclaimed old barn siding and doors for the house, handpicked rocks from their site for the fireplace, and insisted on antique beams for their timber frame home. The lintels supporting the weight of the open fireplace and the cobblestone for the chimneys and granite for the walks were all reclaimed by the owners. In addition to the two main floors, there is a guest suite in the walkout basement with two bedrooms and a sitting room with fireplace.

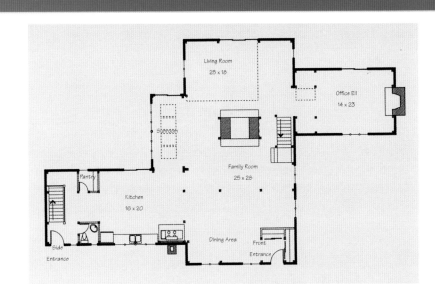

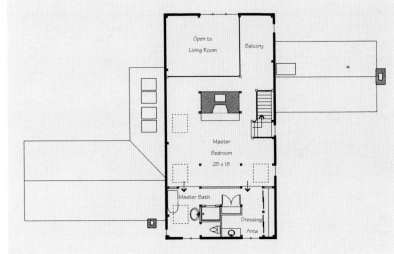

Photo credit: © 1990 Suki Coughlin

A family room and living room flank the enormous fireplace, made from stones the owners selected during site excavation. The family room feels more cozy with the lower ceiling. The living room is a guaranteed wow, soaring two stories high.

An ell was designed specifically for an office for a work-at-homeowner. Like the rest of the home, the appointments are an accumulation of family heirlooms and found antiques.

The pantry doorframe was designed to accommodate a 1740s door, complete with original latch, paint, and seed poster.

An 1898 stove and a slate sink were salvaged from other
homes and enshrined in the kitchen.

Photo credit: © Suki Coughlin

The entire upstairs was devoted to master bedroom and bath.

Two-step Plan

Before fully committing to a
holiday retreat in New Hampshire, two Bostonites decided to
start small and test their commit-
ment. The barn-like cottage they
built ended up enjoying heavy use
— weekends and vacations. So
they went all the way, fully committing with a linked, but very-different
colonial next door to what would
become their guesthouse.

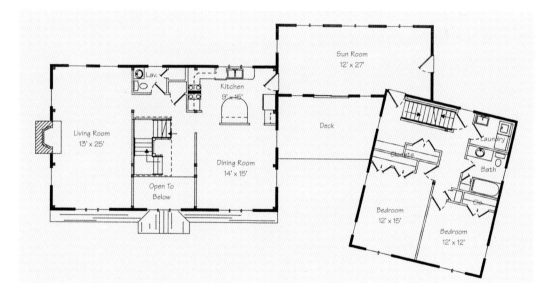

Closet

Bath Clo. Clo.

Library
13' x 21'

Master
Bedroom
14' x 17'

Deck

Deck

Kitchen

Bath

Great Room
24' x 24'

Deck

Lav.

Kitchen
9' x 15'

Sun Room
12' x 27'

Living Room
13' x 25'

Deck

Laundry

Closets

Bath

Clo.

Dining Room
14' x 15'

Open To
Below

Bedroom
12' x 15'

Bedroom
12' x 12'

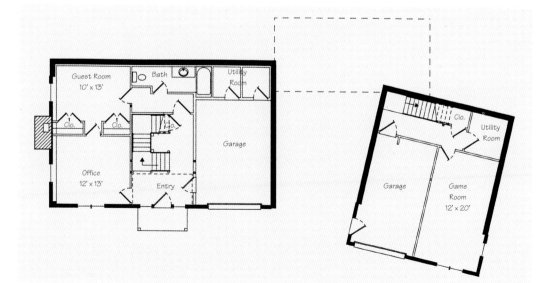

Guest Room
10' x 13'

Bath

Utility
Room

Clo.

Clo.

Clo.

Garage

Utility
Room

Office
12' x 13'

Entry

Garage

Game
Room
12' x 20'

The upstairs area in the guesthouse is an open kitchen and living area.

The homeowners opted against a high ceiling in their living room, designing a more formal space around furniture they already owned. A small breakfast nook in the kitchen gets a lot of use.

The owner's favorite hangout is in their den/library upstairs, off the master bedroom. The best views of the lake are just outside the French doors in the large dormer.

A Jacuzzi tub offers an invitation to kick back and watch clouds drift past the skylight.

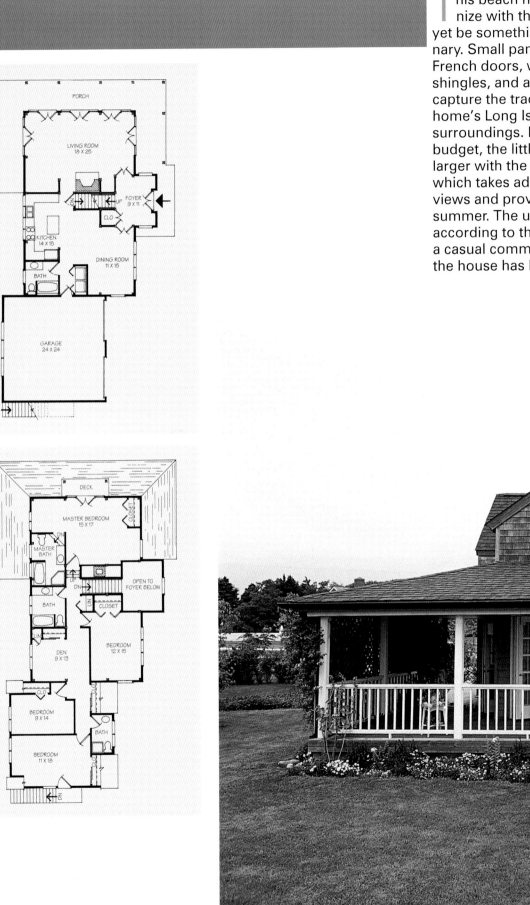

Shore Thing

This beach house had to harmonize with the surrounding area, yet be something out of the ordinary. Small pane windows and French doors, white cedar shingles, and a winged porch capture the traditional style of the home's Long Island, New York surroundings. Built on a small budget, the little house seems larger with the extensive veranda, which takes advantage of ocean views and provides shade in the summer. The ultimate compliment, according to the homeowner, was a casual comment that "it looks like the house has been here forever."

The living is best outdoors during summers at a beach house. This porch was planned and furnished for such use. French doors surround three sides of the living room, opening out onto the veranda.

A traditional carved wood fireplace graces the center of the home.

Recut old beams form interesting angles in the comfortable den.

In the master bedroom, French doors open onto a private deck.

A charming dinner table is set, with inviting padded bench seats filling a corner of the small dining room.

The living room has a raised, 9'4" ceiling for a spacious feel while leaving enough space for living quarters above.

he attractive little sunroom atop this barn-style home is called a "sugar house loft" and, appropriately enough, it offers its dwellers a view of Sugar Loaf Mountain in Maryland. A contractor himself, this homeowner wanted to build his own home using pre-engineered components because he was convinced the quality was generally better than traditional stick-frame houses and because the time of construction was shorter.

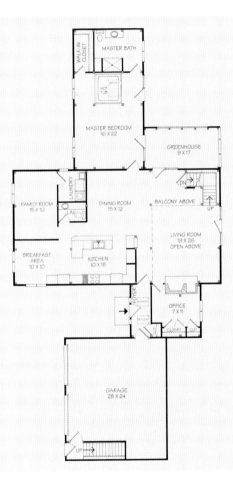

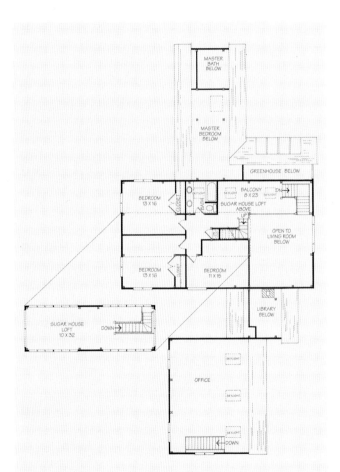

Pages 108 & 109
Left & top right: The living quarters were kept open for a connected feeling among family members in living, cooking, and dining areas. The kitchen opens to the great room through an arched brick facade over the oven range, reminiscent of a Colonial fireplace.

Center right: A sunroom in back is used as an attractive breakfast nook.

Bottom right: The master bedroom suite soars up to the roofline, with track lighting installed along the beams to create a light and airy feeling, even after the sun has set.

Just Beachy

Light colors and lots of light through big glass windows characterize this uncharacteristic timber frame home off Cape Cod. Remotely located, this home had to have a home office, as well as lots of spare bedrooms for guests who travel great distances to visit. By white washing the walls and ceilings and pickling the floors, a light, warm-looking beach house was created.

Sunroom
Above

Bedroom
8 x 10

Playroom
12 x 17

Deck Above

Bath

Up

Bedroom
10 x 10

Hobby Room
10 x 10

Garage
20 x 13

Sunroom
14 x 17

Kitchen
8 x 15

Living Room
15 x 23

Deck

Up

Dn

Den
8 x 16

Bedroom
10 x 11

Bath

Open to
Living Room
Below

Jacuzzi

Bath

Master
Bedroom
13 x 18

Dn

Closet

Up to
Windows
Walk

Catwalk

Office
11 x 10

Photo by Sidney Morris

Pastels were used in the great room to add to the coastal effect.

A fireplace adds charm to the angular master bedroom. Beyond, a
hot tub commands a full view of the shore.

On the mid-level of the home, a bedroom and adjacent den enjoy big windows and skylights. Bold textiles make a statement on bed and furniture.

At the end of a catwalk, high atop the house, sits a home office with such a pleasing view one might be tempted to work!

Photo by Sidney Morris

Photo by Sidney Morris

A sunroom was a logical choice for a beach house, here jutting out on the shore side of the home.

Long Dreamed Of

This homeowner had been envisioning his dream home for years, an ideal home that combined elegant living, classic beauty, and informal formality. The catalyst to making it a reality came when he found a building lot in an exclusive area of Connecticut. The

Photo credit: © Suki Coughlin

Photo credit: © Suki Coughlin

challenge then became creating a home that worked within the elegant ambience of the neighborhood. The result was a colonial with clapboard siding on the outside with an open airy interior made elegant by high ceilings, informal by rough-hewn beams.

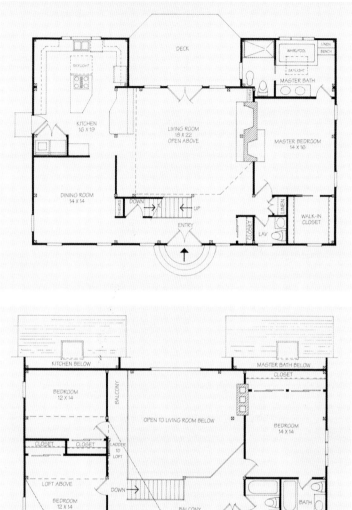

Rich wood tones characterize the adjacent kitchen and dining rooms. Guests in the great/living room can pull up a stool and keep the cook company while she works.

A massive brick chimney allows for fires in both the great room and the master bedroom on the other side.

One of the three guest bedrooms upstairs also serves as home office for the owners.

The master bedroom and bath were tucked downstairs, off the entry foyer.

The Art of Retirement

After a worldly career in art acquisition, living all over Europe, these homeowners elected to retire to New Hampshire. They designed a home that would combine the traditional timber frame with the contemporary stretches of white wall space they needed to display their art collection. They had a lot of other things to display, as well, including tastes for the exotic. So guest rooms were designed and furnished to reflect different countries and regions where they'd lived years before. Their home is like a tour of Europe.

Photo credit: © Suki Coughlin

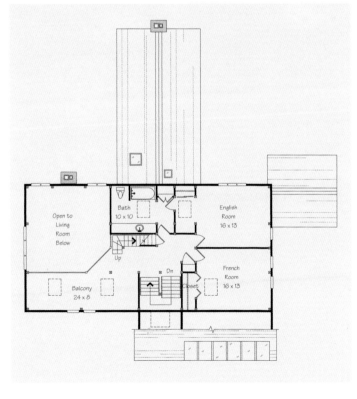

To open up the foyer and achieve an entry reminiscent of European entrance halls, the fireplace was positioned at the side, rather than the center, of the house.

A third floor loft overlooks the living room.

A fireplace fills floor to ceiling, and windows flow around three walls in the master bedroom.

Photo credit: © Suki Coughlin

Photo credit: © Suki Coughlin

Family Ties

An old farm field overlooking a lake proved irresistible to a couple shopping for the ideal vacation site for themselves, their three children, and grandchildren too. Home design was a little harder to visualize, at first. They first considered a log home, but found the timbers overwhelming. They scaled down to timber frame and never looked back.

Porch

Living Room
20 x 24

Bedroom #2
10.5 x 12

Bath

Up

Dining Area
12 x 14

Entry
9 x 10

Kitchen
12 x 14

Mudroom/
Laundry
7 x 13

Clo.

Mechanical Room
7 x 11

Garage
23 x 31

Clo.

Master Bedroom
12.5 x 24

Seat

Shelves

Bath
7 x 16

Storage

Bedroom #3
12 x 12

Clo.

Dn

Open to Below

Bedroom #4
10.5 x 11

Clo.

Bath

Balcony
12 x 14

Unfinished Space
23 x 39

Photo credit: © 1999 Suki Coughlin

Photo credit: © 1999 Suki Coughlin

Pages 128 & 129
Left: The stone fireplace, 10-foot raised ceilings, and French doors with a wrap-around porch were ideas the homeowners had in mind when designing their house.

Top right & bottom right: From the cozy kitchen, the ceiling opens up over a dining area, overlooked by a balcony. Rich wood beams punctuate cream-colored ceiling panels. A light green was used on the walls in the kitchen and dining area to add color and character.

A window seat was a prerequisite for the owner, who wanted to escape to a quiet place where they could enjoy their view.

The second-floor balcony has been furnished with a bed, and stocked with toys — a playroom for frequent visits from grandchildren.

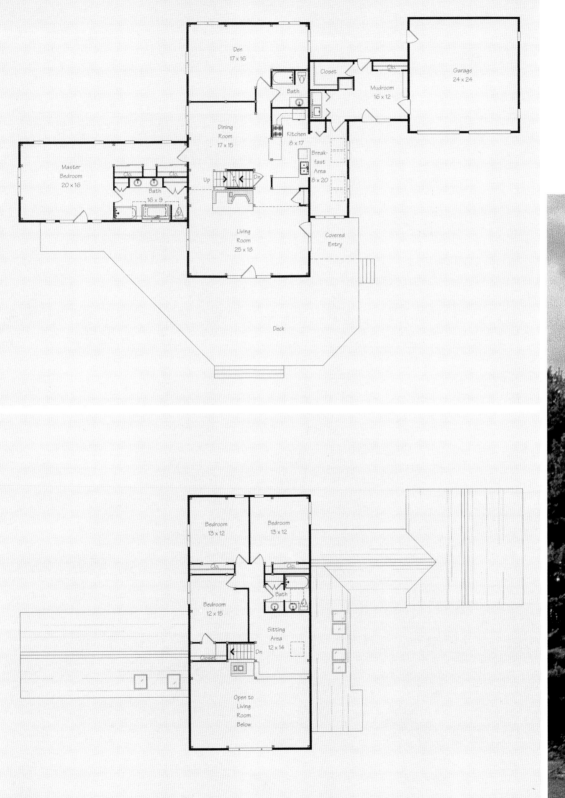

Den
17 x 16

Closet

Bath

Garage
24 x 24

Mudroom
16 x 12

Clo.

Dining
Room
17 x 15

Kitchen
8 x 17

Master
Bedroom
20 x 16

Bath
16 x 9

Up

Dn

Break-
fast
Area
8 x 20

Living
Room
25 x 18

Covered
Entry

Deck

Bedroom
13 x 12

Bedroom
13 x 12

Clo.

Clo.

Bath

Bedroom
12 x 15

Sitting
Area
12 x 14

Closet

Dn

Open to
Living
Room
Below

Wide Open Space

In designing their barn style home, these homeowners didn't want any interference with their big open living room: no balcony or overhangs. Just one room soaring up to a cathedral ceiling. They designed the home with a traditional barn look, using weathered siding and metal roof typical of area barns. But instead of a big sliding door opening into a hayloft, they created a bank of windows that overlooks a nearby mountain. To take advantage of their great room, on the second floor they left a sitting room open to the living room below, slightly; concealed behind a half-wall of bookcases that form a functional railing.

Photo credit: © 1996 Suki Coughlin

Photo credit: © 1996 Suki Coughlin

The brick fireplace and chimney were painted white to accentuate the greatness of the great room. Bright, cozy furnishings assure that the room has a comfortable, intimate feel, whether filled with extended family, or serving as quiet retreat for the occupying couple. The room opens out onto a deck that takes full advantage of a spectacular view.

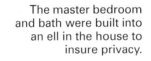

The master bedroom and bath were built into an ell in the house to insure privacy.

A breakfast area is brightened by windows and sliding glass doors.

A Humble Approach

At first glance, this seems a small and unassuming home. Set into a hillside, however, it opens up in the back. Inside you'll find a great room worthy of the name, as well as a surprising richness of light completely unexpected on such a wooded lot.

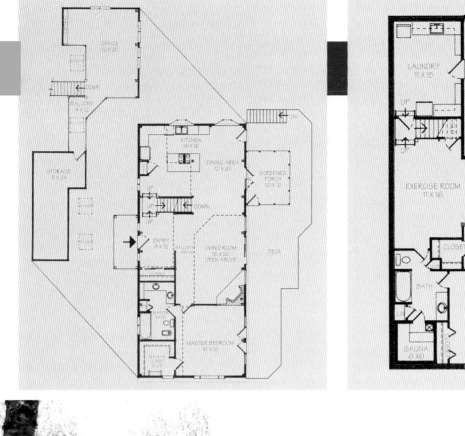

OFFICE
12 X 20

DOWN

BALCONY
4 X 20

STORAGE
8 X 24

KITCHEN
X 16

DINING AREA
10 X 20

SCREENED
PORCH
10 X 12

UP

UP DOWN

UP

ENTRY
8 X 12

BALCONY
ABOVE

LIVING ROOM
16 X 20
OPEN ABOVE

DECK

MASTER BEDROOM
16 X 18

LAUNDRY
11 X 15

GARAGE
12 X 22

MUD ROOM
10 X 12

UP

EXERCISE ROOM
11 X 16

SITTING AREA
10 X 12

UTILITY ROOM
7 X 8

CLOSET

BATH

BEDROOM
14 X 15

SAUNA
6 X 6

The great room opens out to a deck, dappled with light. Inside, the entire home revolves around this one great living space, with balconies and open staircases enjoying view of both living room and the woods beyond.

This cook wanted a modern kitchen that worked with the country charm of the home. The cabinets were finished in a bright, mat blue that draws attention away from appliances.

The master bedroom enjoys a private balcony. Transom windows over French doors maximize the morning light that floods this room daily.

Second Time Around

This home was the second timber frame construction for its owners, who "can't imagine not living with wood." And this won't be their last. No sooner had they put up the second than they went back to the drawing table, putting together ideas for a future retirement home. In the meantime, their new home offers them plenty of living space, in addition to an artists studio upstairs, with plans to move the work area to the garage later.

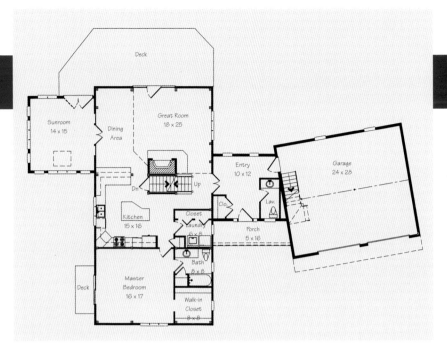

Deck

Sunroom
14 x 15

Dining
Area

Great Room
18 x 25

Entry
10 x 12

Garage
24 x 28

Up

Dn

Closet

Clo.

Lav.

Kitchen
15 x 16

Laundry
6 x 8

Porch
5 x 16

Bath
8 x 8

Deck

Master
Bedroom
16 x 17

Walk-in
Closet
8 x 8

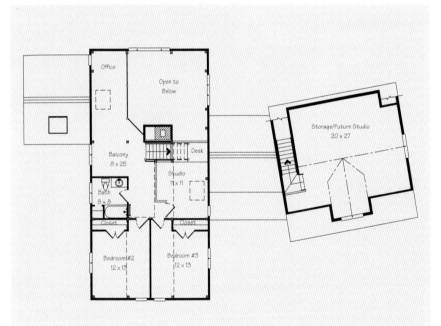

Office

Open to
Below

Storage/Future Studio
20 x 27

Balcony
8 x 25

Desk

Studio
11 x 11

Bath
8 x 8

Closet

Closet

Bedroom #2
12 x 13

Bedroom #3
12 x 13

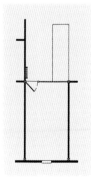

Photo credit: © 1999 Suki Coughlin

Fashioned after an addition they'd put on their previous home, this sunroom offers its owners a light-filled oasis with woodland views in three directions, as well as windows to the sky above.

Sturdy beams provide support so that the Great Room has no
posts or walls to interfere with the open first floor.

Two guest bedrooms were tucked in under the eaves on the second floor, decorated with country antiques and white linens for classic charm.

A large master bedroom has a comfortable sitting area and a private deck accessed through French doors.

For entertaining family and friends, a large country kitchen was designed.

Closet
7 x 8

Master
Bedroom
14 x 17

Bath

Pantry
7 x 8

Nook
6 x 6

Kitchen
10 x 14

Clo.

Great Room
16 x 17

Dining Area
8 x 16

Screen
Porch
10 x 16

Deck

Bedroom
13 x 12

Bedroom
13 x 12

Clo.

Clo.

Study
10 x 12

Bath

Open to
Great Room
Below

Balcony
8 x 22

Not Sticking Out

A couple finds the perfect pastoral site — a meadow, a hilltop, amidst farms in the Connecticut River Valley. How to move onto that hill and enjoy the great views without ruining everyone else's?

This home has actually bought "thank you's" and compliments from the neighbors who overlook it. A large home, it doesn't stand out. And it's real beauty lies in simplicity.

An open kitchen design allows friends to pull up a chair at the island work-station, or to go to the little breakfast nook beyond for more comfortable seating.

This guest bedroom is one of two set aside upstairs for frequent family visits.

A balcony overlooking the living room was set aside as a retreat for reading or watching television.

Opposite page
The open great room is dominated by a fire engine red woodstove, a warm attraction in the winter months.

Photos by Lisanti Photography

Complete with Four C's

Decorator Mary Kraft incorporated
her philosophy of the four
C's — color, coordination, comfort, and convenience — when
working with house designers on

this showpiece. The goal was a sense of cosmopolitan country-living, with elegance in the furnishings and expansiveness in the dimensions.

Photo by Lisanti Photography

A European flavor is cooked up in a kitchen and dining nook with white panels of walls and cabinetry contrasted with dark beams and trim.

Comfort was sacrificed for formal in this elegant dining room, complete with upholstered chairs that invite guests to linger over their meals.

Photo by Lisanti Photography

Top left & center right: Master bedroom and bath are cheerful places, with yellow accents and a stunning plant mural behind the bedstead.

Center left: A nook for television viewing was set aside from the great room.

Bottom right: A home office in the loft is a wonderful escape place, where one can get a little work done, or sneak in a nap.

Photo by Lisanti Photography

Photo credit: © Suki Coughlin

Photo credit: © Suki Coughlin

Disguising an Add-on

Philadelphia city dwellers, this couple was looking for a weekend retreat. What they fell in love with was an old stone home built in 1810. So in love, in fact, that they soon moved to the house. And soon felt squeezed for space, especially since one owner was running her business as a psychiatrist out of the home. A new entrance separates the flow of family to the home and clients to the office. In building an addition, they wanted to keep the historic appearance of the home. By tucking the addition onto the back of the house, they were able to take advantage of the slope of the property, and they gained views that had previously been walled off. Best of all, "The house looks like it's always been together. People don't know the old from the new," the proud owner says.

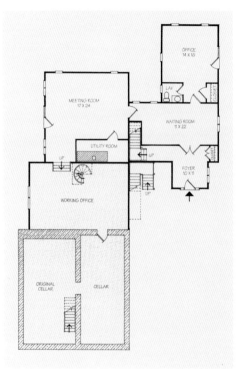

Photo credit: © Suki Coughlin

A spacious master bedroom and bath were two perks gained by building the addition.

A deck between the new master bedroom and living room adds a welcome extension into the outdoors.

With a Buck's County stone fireplace and antique beams, the newly constructed interior appears to have been here for years. A bank of windows opens up a view previously walled off to the homeowners. The space created in the new addition allows the homeowners to host parties of 50 or more people.

By building an addition, the kitchen and dining areas gained greater space in the old building.

Doubling the Space

These homeowners needed a whole lot more room, but they didn't want to give up their historic stone home. A hallway on the ground floor, as well as an overhanging roof now connect to an incredible addition that created a lot more living space for both the occupants and their guests, as well as their vehicles.

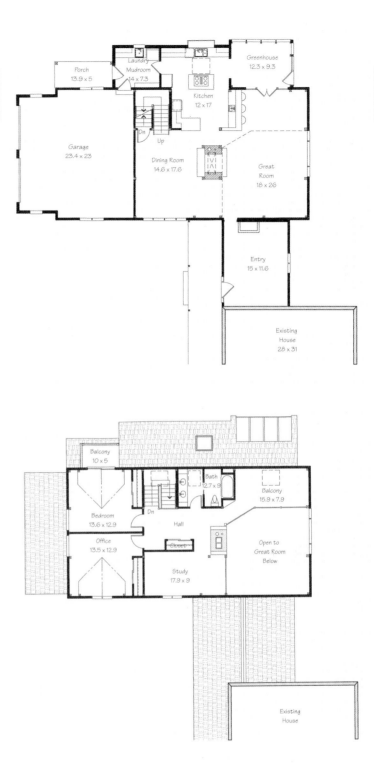

Porch
13.9 x 5

Laundary
Mudroom
14 x 7.3

Greenhouse
12.3 x 9.3

Kitchen
12 x 17

Garage
23.4 x 23

Dn

Up

Dining Room
14.6 x 17.6

Great
Room
18 x 26

Entry
15 x 11.6

Existing
House
28 x 31

Balcony
10 x 5

Bath
12.7 x 9

Balcony
15.9 x 7.9

Bedroom
13.6 x 12.9

Dn

Hall

Office
13.5 x 12.9

Closet

Open to
Great Room
Below

Study
17.9 x 9

Existing
House

Photo by Rob Knight

A sunroom serves as informal breakfast nook off the kitchen.

The new great room circles a massive stone fireplace. Living, dining, and cooking areas are all interconnected, with balconies overlooking both the living space and capitalizing on the light and views from a bank of windows.

Photo by Rob Knight

Front On

These homeowners didn't want a front and a back for their home, they wanted two fronts. They designed a home with a Colonial appearance, graced with oversized windows that maximize view and light. The exterior is two houses in one. As you enter the property, you are greeted with a traditional Colonial house. Enter the house through the front door into a foyer, and you are met with two French doors and a breathtaking view through the dining room's oversized windows to the mountains. Inside, they used high ceilings to create a feeling of spaciousness downstairs, without sacrificing any upstairs room to a cathedral ceiling.

Photo by Rich Frutchey

Garage
24 x 28

Up

Up

Closet

Gallery
16 x 17

Covered
Porch
8 x 16

Pantry

D
W

Bath
7.5 x 9

Kitchen
14 x 16

Dn

Up

Foyer
9 x 11

Dining Room
16 x 20

Living Room
20 x 30

Storage
Loft
24 x 27

Dn

Bedroom
16 x 26

Bath
7.5 x 9

Bedroom
15 x 16

Open to
Below

Dn

Closet

Bath
9 x 14

Sunroom
16 x 20

Closet
9 x 10

Closet
9 x 9

Master
Bedroom
20 x 20

Photo by Rich Frutchey

Photo by Rich Frutchey

Photo by Rich Frutchey

Top left, center left & top center: Wide hallways and 10-foot ceilings create a feeling of spaciousness. The rooms downstairs flow one to the next through French doors.

Traditional in design, this room gets a modern facelift with oversize windows that maximize light and view, while conserving energy using the latest insulating technology.

Photo by Rich Frutchey

Photo by Rich Frutchey

Photo by Rich Frutchey

Top right & bottom right: Upstairs, dormers and a raised room allow the master bedroom suite, a sunroom, and two guestrooms to take full advantage of breathtaking mountain views.

Photo by Rich Frutchey

Photo by Rich Frutchey

Photo by Rich Frutchey

Many Points of View

With a mountain lot, priority number one was to enjoy the view. So the designer worked to take advantage of the views while gaining southern exposure in the winter and avoiding the hot summer sun to the west. Window placement was critical, because the homeowners wanted almost every room to share stock in the view.

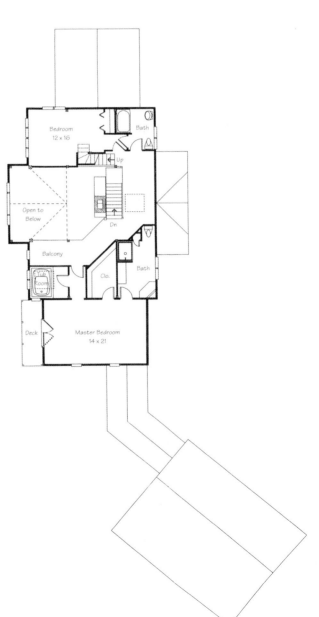

Even the Jacuzzi was to share in the mountainous view, so by placing it in its own room on the second floor, a private entrance to the master bedroom was created. Planned as a retirement home, the owners made sure there was a bedroom on the first floor should they ever need it.

Opposite page
All the main living areas of the house connect to the great room, dominated by a massive stone fireplace and chimney in the center of the home.

The kitchen and dining areas are connected, allowing the hostess to cook and converse with guests at the same time.

Wooded from View

Tucked back from a secondary road, in the midst of cool woods, this home is a sanctuary for former city dwellers who wanted to retire away from the rat race.

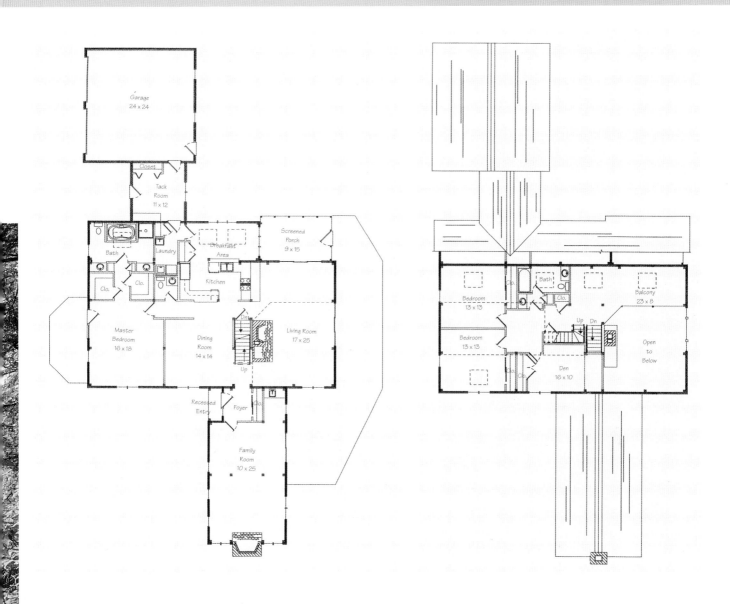

Roof trusses over the central structure allow for a great room that soars up, unencumbered by supports below.

The homeowner enjoys cooking, and a large kitchen was included in the plans to allow her to experiment.

A ground-floor master bedroom and bath were tucked into an ell for privacy and convenience.

Country Elegance

T his mountain retreat was designed to take in panoramic views. There is no front and back – each face of the home presents an attractive yet unobtrusive facade. The inside is even more attractive, with views from charmingly decorated rooms to the soft, mountainous horizons beyond.

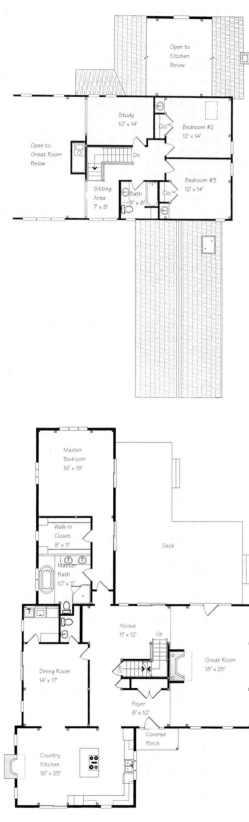

Open to
Kitchen
Below

Study
10' x 14'

Clo.

Bedroom #2
12' x 14'

Open to
Great Room
Below

Dn

Bedroom #3
12' x 14'

Sitting
Area
7 x 8'

Bath
8' x 8'

Clo.

Master
Bedroom
16' x 18'

Walk-in
Closet
8' x 11'

Deck

Master
Bath
10' x 11'

Alcove
11' x 12'

Up

Great Room
18' x 25'

Dining Room
14' x 17'

Foyer
8' x 10'

Covered
Porch

Country
Kitchen
16' x 25'

The great room is delicately furnished with floral upholstery for a feminine feel that complements the antique porcelain on display.

A big jacuzzi offers occupants a view of the clouds as they soak away their cares.

The master bedroom opens to a private deck. A comfortable check couch makes this room a quiet retreat when the house is full of family and guests.

An informal sitting area was positioned adjacent to the kitchen, where everyone tends to congregate. A fire and comfy chairs invite guests to linger and keep the cook company.

Photo credit: © Suki Coughlin

Photo credit: © 1994 Suki Coughlin

Budget Conscious

Because this Florida couple would only use their New Hampshire home during the summer, they didn't need a big home, and they tied themselves to a small lot and a little budget to set the limits. They extended their living space with less expensive outdoor space, such as a screen porch and decks. And they didn't provide the most spacious guest bedrooms. Still, they got all the living space they wanted, including a third-floor loft studio, and office space overlooking the living room.

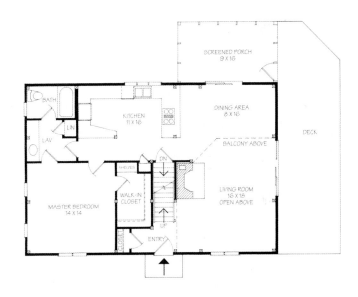

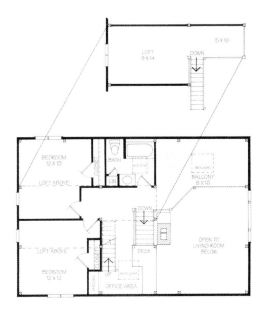

Though the home was kept small, the living room was allowed to be great, with a cathedral ceiling and an impressive bank of windows.

To keep the kitchen from feeling hemmed in, a wall of cabinets was built so that the rest of the room could remain open.

Bonus space: a sitting area in a loft overlooks the living room.

No Walls

There are no interior walls in the central living quarters of this home, nothing to block the 360-degree views of the Shenandoah Valley on one side, the Blue Ridge Mountains on the other. The homeowners chose antique timber to support this wide-open view. "We didn't want to sit in a new home and listen to new timbers checking and cracking as they shrink," they said. When they took their house plans to the site, they realized they wanted more windows and even fewer walls, so they went back to the drawing table. They also drew in their furniture to see how it would fit, and ended up bumping out the living room wall so that they could more easily accommodate doors under the arched window.

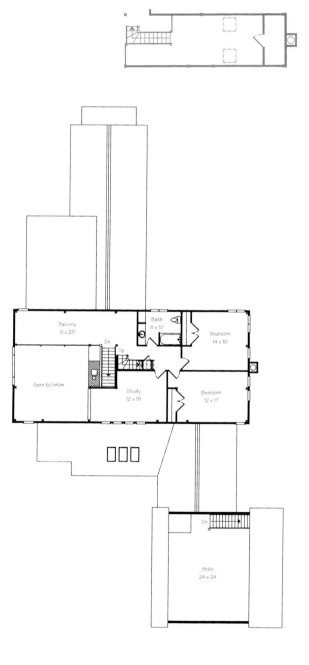

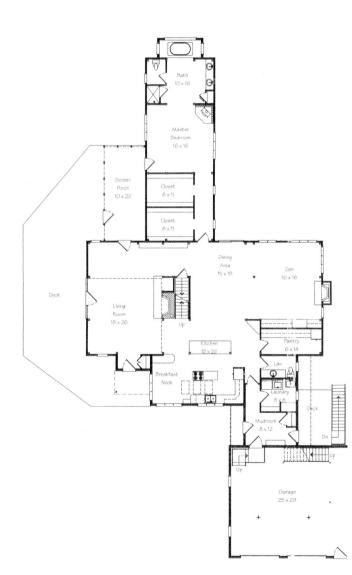

A cathedral ceiling and soaring windows characterize the great room of this home. Stairways and balconies capitalize on the views, winding their way round a fieldstone fireplace.

The homeowner designed her kitchen based on a picture she'd seen in a magazine.

The homeowners based their new master bath on the design they had in their old home. They wanted the master bedroom on the first floor, so an ell was built to accommodate the private quarters.

A cozy den was built off the
dining room.